Another Place

GENERAL EDITORS

Karl G. Heider & Frank Cancian

ANOTHER PLACE

Photographs of a Maya Community

Frank Cancian

Scrimshaw Press

1974

Cancian, Frank
Another place ; photographs of a Maya community.

Includes bibliographical references
1. Tzotzil Indians—Pictorial works.   2. Zinacantán,
Mexico—Social life and customs—Pictorial works.
I. Title.
F1221.T9C29   1974   970.3   74-1227
ISBN 0-912020-33-4
ISBN 0-912020-34-2 (pbk.)

The Scrimshaw Press
149 Ninth Street
San Francisco CA 94103

THE PEOPLE IN THIS BOOK are Zinacantecos. Their community, Zinacantan, includes more than a dozen hamlets spread over highland valleys and hillsides in southeastern Mexico. Inside this community they maintain a distinctive way of life. It binds them together. And it sets them apart from other Indians and from the non-Indian population that dominates the nearby city of San Cristobal de las Casas. Outside their community, in the city and on the lands they rent and farm, they and other Indians share the disadvantages of being both poor and low in the ethnic hierarchy.

In their own eyes they are Zinacantecos first, Indians second, and Mexicans last, if at all. At home, they shuck the oppression of the larger world and elevate themselves in relation to economically less successful Indians in nearby communities. They build a nearly-complete universe within themselves, finding good and bad, religious and irreligious, rich and poor, industrious and lazy among the 10,000 people who are Zinacantecos.

Most of the usual and unusual features of Zinacanteco life and customs have been described in detail by anthropologists. They weave with backstrap looms, carry with tumplines. Men wear colorful ribbons on their hats, red and white striped tops and short pants; they carry made-in-Hartford machetes when they go to their cornfields. Women pat out countless tortillas and always walk behind men. Chickens are sacrificed to Maya gods under crosses on a mountain-top overlooking the Catholic church. A proper meal is preceded by rinsing out the mouth as well as hand-washing and Zinacantecos die easily of measles, a European disease.

Having spent three of the last thirteen years doing anthropological research among Zinacantecos, I know that these and similar things provide the form for daily life. But they really make very little difference. Zinacantan is another place where people live.

To Juan Vásquez

19

21

24

FIESTAS TO CELEBRATE THE SAINTS bring people from all hamlets together in the religious and political center. The fifty men who sponsor fiestas each year spend many times their annual earnings for liquor, food, costumes and fireworks and they commit themselves and their families and assistants to weeks of preparations for rituals. In return, they receive enduring prestige in the community, the satisfaction of religious service, and the excitement of being in the middle of the most important public events of the year.

27

28

29

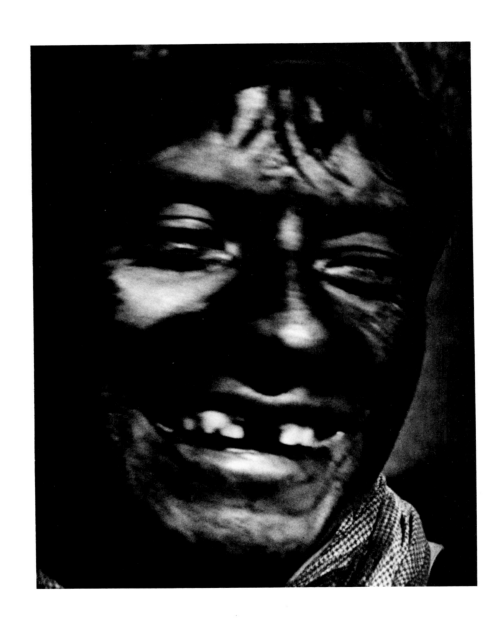

38

ZINACANTECOS and more than 150,000 Indians from other towns support the commercial life of San Cristobal. Zinacantecos go there often to shop, sell agricultural products and enjoy a day in the city. Less frequently they go to consult the doctors, lawyers and priests who live there. Relations with city people are better now than they were a generation ago when Indians were often jailed for being in the city after dark.

41

43

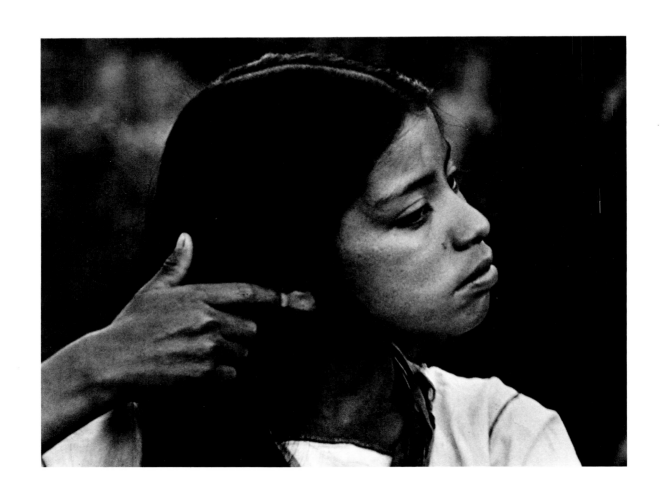

IN THE HOT, BUGGY LOWLANDS men live in temporary shelters, cook their own food, and look forward to the time they can return home. They produce corn and beans, take them home on pack animals, clean and prepare them for market, and sit in the San Cristobal marketplace selling directly to the consumer. The rocky, hilly land they rent makes mechanized farming difficult, but roads, trucks and government-sponsored wholesaling facilities have recently changed the way they transport and market their products.

Change is frequent in Zinacanteco life. It was only twenty-five or thirty years ago that land reform broke up lowland estates and transformed the great majority of Zinacantecos from peons to independent peasant farmers.

56

1961

1961

1971

LOCAL JUDGES SETTLE DISPUTES at the municipal building in Zinacantan center and officials from outside also meet groups of citizens there. Zinacantan is formally organized like all other *municipios* in the state of Chiapas, but local officials are chosen according to local traditions. Judges hear out all parties to disputes and aim at mediation that will maintain good relations in the community.

65

69

1971

CURERS PRAY AT THE CHURCH and at the four sacred mountains surrounding Zinacantan center. They offer incense, candles and liquor to the gods and concentrate on restoring good relations between the sick person and the supernatural. Crosses mark the "entrances" to the mountains and Maya souls live within them. Most Zinacantecos use modern drugs to supplement native curing, but they rarely visit doctors.

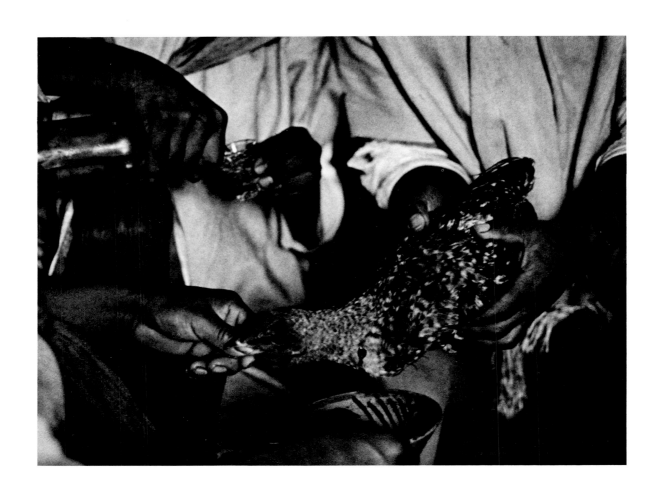

82

Acknowledgements

MOST OF THESE PHOTOGRAPHS were made in Summer 1971 when I went to Zinacantan to devote myself exclusively to taking pictures. Some were made in the course of anthropological fieldwork in 1961 and 1962. In 1970-71, the Center for Advanced Study in the Behavioral Sciences provided the lifespace necessary to plan the book. The Wenner-Gren Foundation for Anthropological Research and the Latin American Studies Program at Stanford University provided financial aid for Summer 1971.

It is a pleasure finally to acknowledge encouragement given by David McAllester, Sam Green and the late Edward Steichen more than fifteen years ago, and by Francesca Cancian for the last fifteen years. Her sense of adventure has helped at almost every stage of the work.

My greatest debt is to the people of Zinacantan, especially those in the photographs on the preceding pages. I want to record thanks to the families of Juan and Pedro Vásquez, the late Pedro Pérez con Dios and Juan Sánchez Vásquez in Navenchauc, Antonio Vásquez in Pih, José Hernández Nuh in Nachig and Domingo de la Torre Pérez in Zinacantan center, and to Marcos Pérez Gonzáles, *presidente municipal* during 1971, and to his fellow officials.

Brief Bibliography

Vogt, Evon Z. *Zinacantan: A Maya Community in the Highlands of Chiapas.* Cambridge, 1969.
  (A rich, detailed book)
Vogt, Evon Z. *The Zinacantecos of Mexico: A Modern Maya Way of Life.* New York, 1970.
  (A widely available paperback overview)

More specialized studies

Blaffer, Sarah C. *The Black-man of Zinacantan: A Central American Legend.* Austin, 1972.
Bricker, Victoria R. *Ritual Humor in Highland Chiapas.* Austin, 1973.
Cancian, Francesca M. *What Are Norms? A Study of Beliefs and Action in a Maya Community.*
  New York, forthcoming.
Cancian, Frank. *Economics and Prestige in a Maya Community: The Religious Cargo System in
  Zinacantan.* Stanford, 1965.
Cancian, Frank. *Change and Uncertainty in a Peasant Economy: The Maya Corn Farmers of
  Zinacantan.* Stanford, 1972.
Collier, George A. *Man and Land in Highland Chiapas: The Ecological Basis of Tzotzil Tradition.*
  Austin, forthcoming.
Collier, Jane. *Law and Social Change in Zinacantan.* Stanford, 1973.

Printing: Cal Central Press, February 1974
Composition: Monotype Spectrum by Mackenzie & Harris
Paper: Warren's Flokote | Binding: Cardoza-James
Typography: Frederick Mitchell
Design: Frank Cancian